Zoom In on
Desert Animals

Iguanas

Leo Statts

abdopublishing.com

Published by Abdo Zoom™, PO Box 398166, Minneapolis, Minnesota 55439. Copyright © 2017 by Abdo Consulting Group, Inc. International copyrights reserved in all countries. No part of this book may be reproduced in any form without written permission from the publisher. Abdo Zoom™ is a trademark and logo of Abdo Consulting Group, Inc.

Printed in the United States of America, North Mankato, Minnesota
062016
092016

THIS BOOK CONTAINS RECYCLED MATERIALS

Cover Photo: Shutterstock Images
Interior Photos: Shutterstock Images, 1, 9, 12; Maciej Czekajewski/Shutterstock Images, 5; Kenta Studio/Shutterstock Images, 6; Don Mammoser/Shutterstock Images, 7; Olga Utlyakova/iStockphoto, 8; iStockphoto, 10–11; Red Line Editorial, 11, 20 (left), 20 (right), 21 (left), 21 (right); Tony Moran/Shutterstock Images, 13; JHVEPhoto/Shutterstock Images, 14; Bluedog Studio/Shutterstock Images, 16; Patrick K. Campbell/Shutterstock Images, 17; Alberto Loyo/Shutterstock Images, 19

Editor: Brienna Rossiter
Series Designer: Madeline Berger
Art Direction: Dorothy Toth

Publisher's Cataloging-in-Publication Data
Names: Statts, Leo, author.
Title: Iguanas / by Leo Statts.
Description: Minneapolis, MN : Abdo Zoom, [2017] | Series: Desert animals | Includes bibliographical references and index.
Identifiers: LCCN 2016941143 | ISBN 9781680791815 (lib. bdg.) | ISBN 9781680793499 (ebook) | ISBN 9781680794380 (Read-to-me ebook)
Subjects: LCSH: Iguanas--Juvenile literature.
Classification: DDC 597.95--dc23
LC record available at http://lccn.loc.gov/2016941143

Table of Contents

Iguanas 4

Body 6

Habitat 10

Food 14

Life Cycle 16

Quick Stats 20

Glossary 22

Booklinks 23

Index 24

Iguanas

Iguanas are **reptiles**. Some iguanas live in water. Others live on land. Some people keep them as pets.

Body

An iguana's **scales** can be bright colors.

They can also be tan or gray.

Iguanas have long tails. The tails help them balance and swim.

Iguanas are good swimmers.

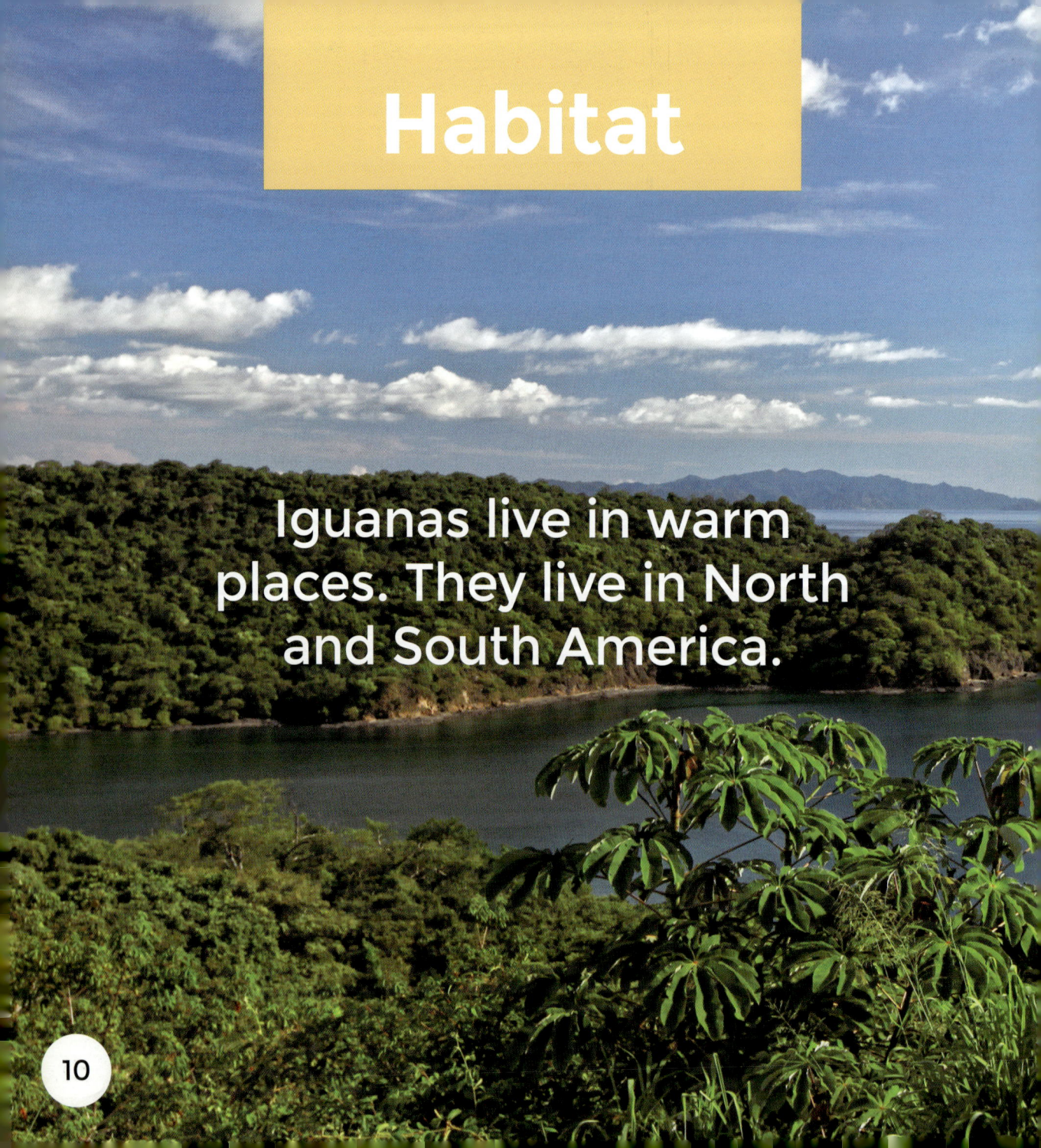

Habitat

Iguanas live in warm places. They live in North and South America.

▢ Where iguanas live

Some iguanas live in **deserts**.

Many live in **rain forests**. They climb high up in trees.

Food

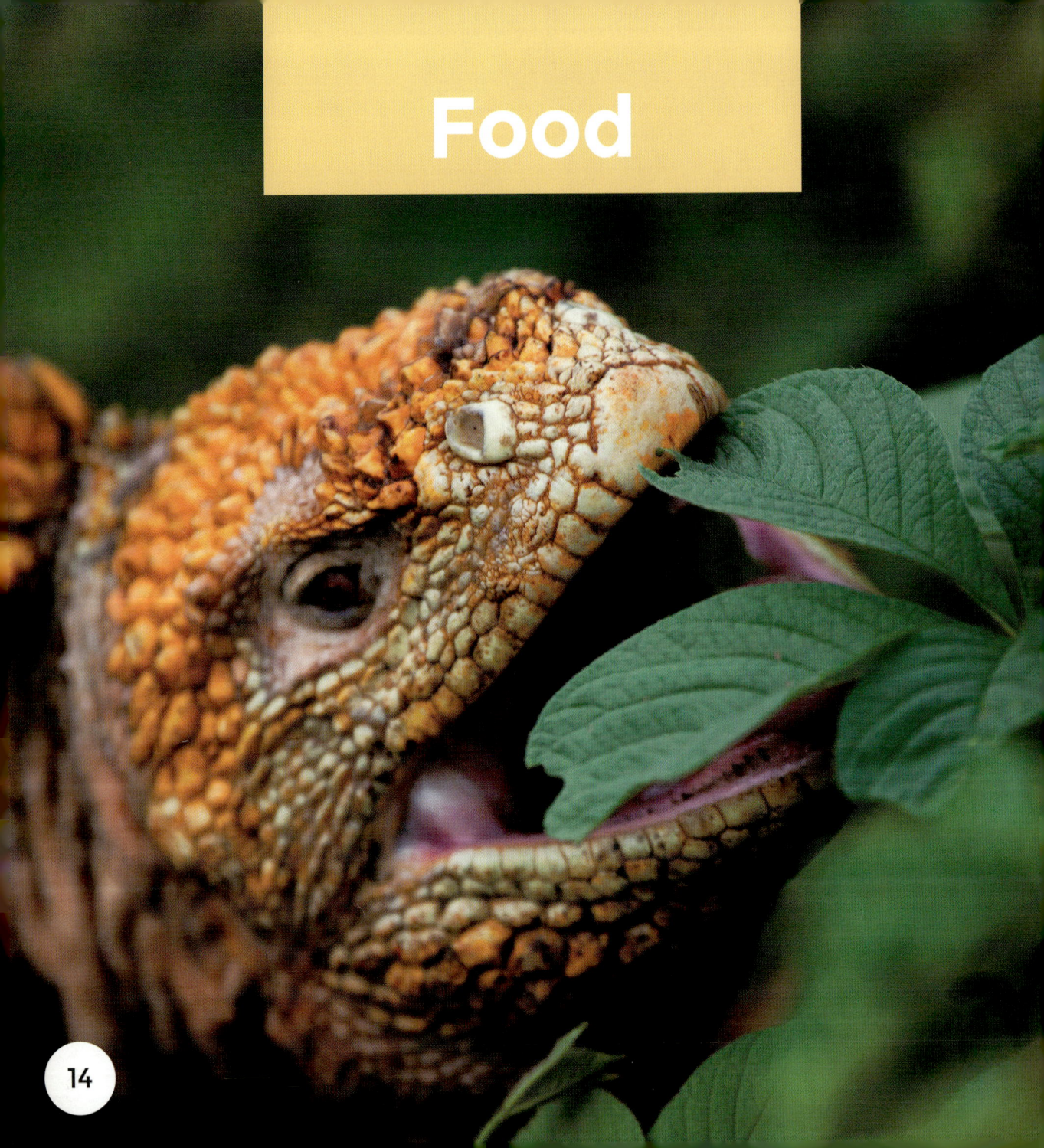

14

Iguanas eat fruit and leaves.
Young iguanas eat
insects and spiders, too.

Life Cycle

Female iguanas lay eggs.
Baby iguanas **hatch** from the eggs.

The babies live on their own.
They find new homes.

There are many kinds of iguanas.
They have different life spans.
Some kinds live for just four years.
Other kinds can live 60 years.

Quick Stats

Average Length – Longest

A green iguana is almost as long as a sofa.

6 ft   7 ft

Average Weight – Heaviest

A blue iguana is as heavy as two bowling balls.

30 lbs   30 lbs

Glossary

desert - a very dry, sandy area with little plant growth.

hatch - to be born from an egg.

rain forest - a tropical woodland where it rains a lot.

reptile - a cold-blooded animal with scales. They typically lay eggs.

scales - flat plates that form the outer covering of reptiles and fish.

Booklinks

For more information on **iguanas**, please visit booklinks.abdopublishing.com

 In on Animals!

Learn even more with the Abdo Zoom Animals database. Check out **abdozoom.com** for more information.

Index

climb, 13

colors, 6

deserts, 12

eggs, 16

pets, 4

rain forests, 13

scales, 6

South America, 10

swim, 8

tails, 8

Edison Twp. Pub. Library
340 Plainfield Ave.
Edison N.J. 08817

APR 03 2017